If the tiara fits

JESS CASTLE
& ESTHER MILTON

Big mouth

THE DEFINITION

OF BEING A *diva*

DO YOU IDENTIFY WITH ANY OF THESE **BUZZWORDS?** IF SO, YOU MAY BE A **TOTAL DIVA.** PERUSE THE PAGES OF THIS BOOK TO FIND MORE *high-maintenance* MUSINGS AND **MANTRAS.**

- **EXTRA** – OVER THE TOP FABULOUSNESS

- **FLAWLESS** – PURE PERFECTION

- **HIGH MAINTENANCE** – THE DIVA WAY

- **KWEEN** – RULER OF ALL THAT GLITTERS

- **O.O.T.D.** – OUTFIT OF THE DAY

- **SASS** – THE DIVA'S PREFERRED MODE OF COMMUNICATION

- **SMIZE** – SMILING WITH THE EYES

- **SLAY** - TO PULL SOMETHING OFF LIKE A BOSS

- **DILEMMA** - WHEN A DIVA HAS TO COMPROMISE

- **DIVA** - AN EXTRA, FLAWLESS, HIGH-MAINTENANCE, SASSY, SLAYIN' KWEEN

WORDS I'D ADD TO THE *Diva Dictionary:*

_____

_____

_____

_____

_____

_____

_____

LET'S **TALK** ABOUT ME. HERE ARE SOME **THINGS** PEOPLE MIGHT NOT KNOW . . .

_____

_____

_____

_____

_____

_____

_____

_____

_____

_____

_____

#HUMBLEBRAG
#BORNFABULOUS
#LIFEOFADIVA

HERE ARE SOME THINGS EVERYONE KNOWS – BECAUSE A **DIVA** LIKES TO SHARE HER *fabulousness*...

#O.T.T.

_____

_____

_____

_____

_____

_____

_____

_____

#LOUDANDPROUD

#ILOVEBEINGEXTRA

RISING

AND shining

(LIKE THE STAR I AM)

REASONS FOR GETTING UP IN THE MORNING:

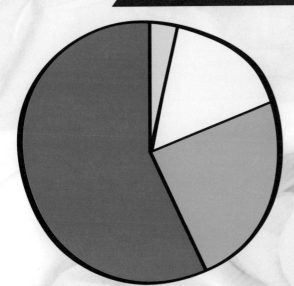

☐ SOMEONE IS GOING TO COOK ME BREAKFAST

☐ SOMEONE IS GOING TO PAY ME TO GET UP (A GIRL CAN DREAM)

☐ THERE'S A SALE GOING ON AND I NEED TO BE FIRST IN LINE

☐ COFFEE

#I woke up like this

#FLAWLESS

WHEN I HIT THE **SNOOZE** BUTTON ON MY ALARM AGAIN . . . AND AGAIN . . . AND AGAIN . . . AND THEN I'M **LATE!**

#SNOOZEFEST

#NOTAMORNINGPERSON

TIMES I'VE TURNED UP *fashionably late:*

_____
_____
_____
_____
_____
_____
_____

MY *favorite* EXCUSES:

_____
_____
_____
_____
_____
_____

#WORTHTHEWAIT

THINGS THAT ARE CRUCIAL
to my AESTHETIC:

ADD MORE HERE.

- ☐ A MATTE LIP
- ☐ STATEMENT EYEBROWS
- ☐ CONTOURING
- ☐ CAREFULLY CONSTRUCTED BED HAIR
- ☐ A TROUTPOUT OR DUCKFACE
- ☐ AN INTENSE SMIZE
- ☐ AN ADORABLE SNAPCHAT FILTER

- ☐ _____
- ☐ _____
- ☐ _____
- ☐ _____
- ☐ _____
- ☐ _____
- ☐ _____

PEOPLE THAT **INSPIRE** MY LOOK:

PEOPLE WHOSE INNER BEAUTY I ADMIRE:

MY *make-up* BAG IS BEING HELD FOR ➤➤➤ **RANSOM** AND I CAN ONLY KEEP **ONE** ITEM.

WHAT **CAN'T I** LIVE WITHOUT?

WRITE HERE.

MY *closet* IS ON **:FIRE:** AND I CAN ONLY SAVE *one item.*

What do I choose?

WRITE HERE.

I'M CHOSEN TO **SING** ON STAGE WITH MY *favorite artist,* AND ONLY HAVE A *minute* TO PREPARE. WHAT DO I PRIORITIZE?

☐ *hair*

☐ *make-up*

☐ *outfit*

BUT **NONE** OF THESE SITUATIONS WOULD SCARE ME *because . . .* I WOKE UP #FLAWLESS

A DIVA'S GUIDE TO:

:LEAVING:

THE house

LEAVING THE HOUSE CAN BE A **MINEFIELD** FOR *high-maintenance* HUMANS.

REMEMBER THESE KEY THINGS TO AVERT A CRISIS:

- ☐ BORING STUFF – KEYS, I.D., ETC.

- ☐ MONEY – THE URGE TO SPLURGE CAN HIT ANYTIME

- ☐ PHONE – AND IT BETTER BE CHARGED!

- ☐ A SNACK – YOU DON'T WANT TO SEE ME WHEN I'M HANGRY

- ☐ NAIL KIT – THIS IS BASIC STUFF, PEOPLE

- ☐ HAND SANITIZER – IN CASE I HAVE TO TOUCH ANYTHING

- ☐ INVISIBLE TIARA – P.S. DON'T FORGET TO STRAIGHTEN IT!

MY OTHER HANDBAG *essentials:*

_____

_____

_____

_____

_____

MY HANDBAG, A.K.A.

#BOTTOMLESSPIT

#I'MSODONE

THAT MOMENT WHEN . . .

I REACH INTO MY HANDBAG TO *discover* THAT MY **COCONUT** WATER HAS **LEAKED.**

#UGH #GIRLBYE

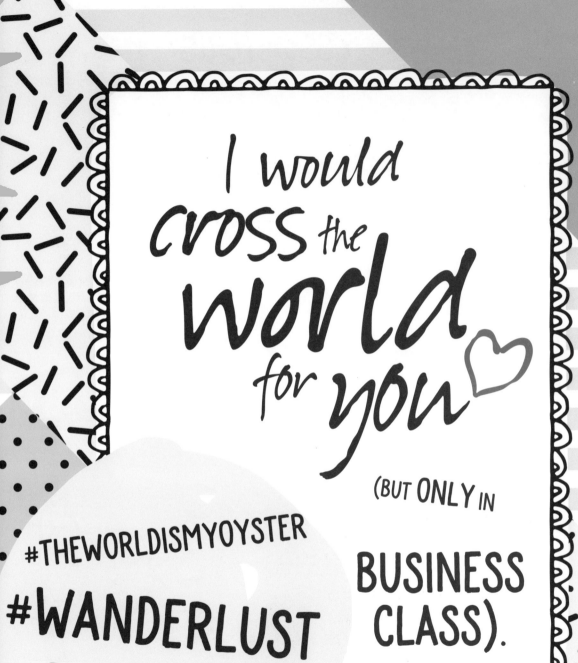

I would cross the world for you ♡

(BUT ONLY IN BUSINESS CLASS).

#THEWORLDISMYOYSTER

#WANDERLUST

#FIRSTCLASSDIVA

HOW TO TRAVEL IN *style:*

- ☐ COERCE MY TRAVEL COMPANION INTO GIVING ME THEIR SHARE OF THE LUGGAGE ALLOWANCE.

- ☐ USE ONE BAG FOR CLOTHES, AND THEN LEAVE THE OTHER EMPTY SO THAT I CAN BRING BACK NEW PURCHASES!

- ☐ SHOW UP LATE BUT CONVINCE THE AIRLINE TO UPGRADE ME TO A BETTER SEAT.

- ☐ JUST BECAUSE SOMEONE SAYS THEY'RE NOT AN ATTENDANT, DOESN'T MEAN THEY CAN'T CARRY MY STUFF.

- ☐ SNEAK INTO THE BUSINESS CLASS LOUNGE AND EAT ALL THE FANCY FOOD.

- ☐ WEAR HUGE SUNGLASSES TO HIDE THE JETLAG... BUT PRETEND TO BE A CELEB GOING INCOGNITO.

- ☐ ORDER A DRINK WITH LOTS OF ICE, AND THEN USE THE ICE FOR MY UNDER-EYE BAGS. FREE BEAUTY TREATMENT!

- ☐ VISIT MY FRIENDS WITH WORSE SEATS TO MAKE SURE THEY KNOW WHAT THEY'RE MISSING.

- ☐ PRETEND TO BE SICK AS WE TOUCH DOWN ON THE RUNWAY SO THAT I GET TO EXIT FIRST.

- ☐ BEDAZZLE MY BAGS SO THEY'RE UNMISTAKABLE ON THE LUGGAGE CAROUSEL.

WHILE WE'RE ON THE SUBJECT OF **TRAVEL,** SOLVE THESE DIVA DILEMMAS **TO CREATE THE PERFECT** ★ ★ ★ ★ ★ VACAY.

SUNBURN IS SO BASIC. HOW DO I ACHIEVE A *gorgeous glow* WITHOUT LOOKING LIKE AN ORANGE CHEETO?

I BOOKED A **5-STAR ACCOMMODATION,** BUT IT'S NOT ACCEPTABLE. WHAT SHOULD I DO?

I WAKE UP **10 MINUTES** BEFORE THE *breakfast* BUFFET ENDS. WHAT DO I DO?

I'VE PURCHASED **MORE** THAN I CAN **FIT** IN MY *luggage.* WHAT DO I **SACRIFICE** FOR THE JOURNEY **HOME?**

IF I **CAN'T** GIVE UP ANYTHING, *how* CAN I *carry it* ALL?

CIRCLE **FIVE** WORDS THAT DESCRIBE THE *perfect* BESPOKE TRAVEL EXPERIENCE.

EXOTIC

SHOPPING

CRUISE

LUXURY

CITY

ART

MICHELIN STAR RESTAURANTS

Reading time

Spa

CLUBS

BEACH

RELAXING

SIGHTSEEING

SNOW

HISTORY

CHAUFFEUR

SPORTS

PARTY

PEACEFUL

Pamper

Countryside

EXCITING

CULTURE

AUTHENTIC STREETFOOD

Glamping

Exclusive

A DIVA'S GUIDE TO:

BEING A SOCIAL MEDIA kween

THEY AREN'T CALLED FOLLOWERS FOR **NOTHING**.
I RULE MY E-EMPIRE WITH THESE DIVA DOs & DON'Ts!

DO

☐ SHOW OFF MY FABULOUS LIFE

☐ DAZZLE EVERYONE WITH MY WIT

☐ SPY ON MY EX FROM A HEALTHY DISTANCE

☐ THANK MY LOYAL SUBJECTS EVERY ONCE IN A WHILE

☐ START REFERRING TO MY SOCIAL MEDIA STYLE AS MY "BRAND"

DON'T

☐ ENGAGE WITH TROLLS

☐ OVERDO THE HASHTAGS #OVERKILL

☐ SPAM MY FEED. I WOULDN'T EAT IT, SO DON'T POST IT

☐ POST ANYTHING I WOULDN'T WANT MY MOTHER TO SEE

☐ MAKE MYSELF RELATABLE – I'M NOT HERE TO BE ORDINARY!

TIMES I WISHED THERE WAS AN "**UNDO**" BUTTON I.R.L.:

WHEN I ACCIDENTLY LIKE SOMEONE'S PHOTO FROM **THREE** MONTHS ★ AGO . . .

MIPHONE PROBS #2

PEOPLE WHOSE **SOCIAL MEDIA** I CHECK ON **MORE** THAN MY OWN:

#UBERFAN

_____

_____

#LOVETHEM _____

#INSPO _____

MY *social media* STYLE IS **MAINLY...**

TRENDY & TOPICAL

I KNOW WHAT'S GOING TO TREND BEFORE A HASHTAG HAS EVEN BEEN INVENTED FOR IT.

ALOOF & OFF-LINE

I RARELY POST BUT WHEN I GET TAGGED BY SOMEONE, I GET MILLIONS OF LIKES. I WON'T MESSAGE YOU BACK THOUGH.

FASHIONABLE & FLEEK

I'M THE ONE THAT COINS NAMES FOR NEW HAIR COLORS. MY O.O.T.D. IS ALWAYS ON POINT.

HAPPY & HEALTHY

I LOVE SHARING INSPIRATIONAL PICS AND QUOTES THAT SPREAD POSITIVITY.

SARCASTIC & SASSY

NOTHING I SAY SHOULD BE TAKEN SERIOUSLY. YOU CAN COUNT ON ME FOR FUNNY MEMES AND SASSY COMMENTS.

ADD MORE HERE.

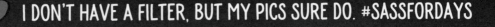

I DON'T HAVE A FILTER, BUT MY PICS SURE DO. #SASSFORDAYS

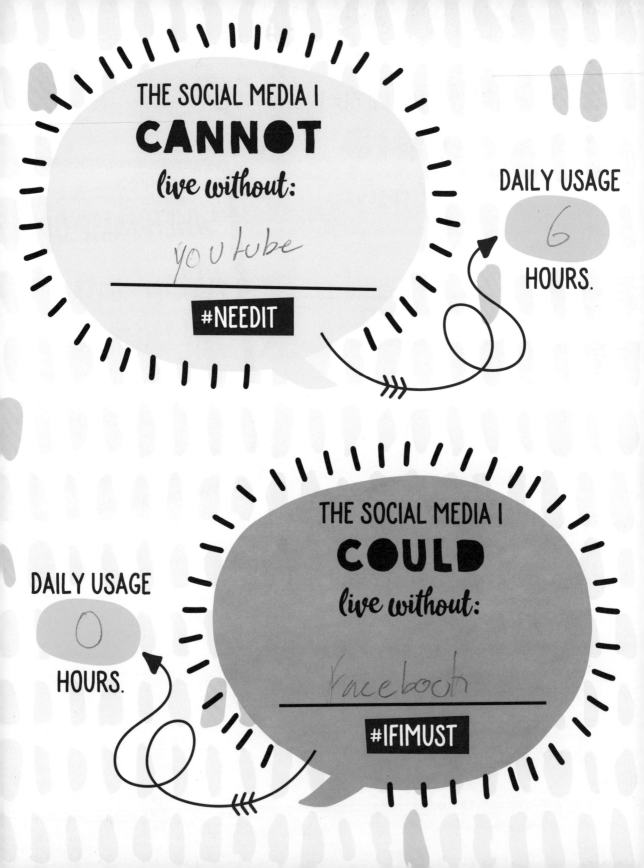

THE SOCIAL MEDIA I
AVOID
at all costs:

_____

#OVERIT

WHEN I USE UP
ALL MY DATA . . .
IN THE FIRST
WEEK.

MIPHONE PROBS #3

WHAT I WOULD DO IF
social media HAD
NEVER
BEEN
INVENTED:

#SOLASTCENTURY

_____

_____

_____

_____

REASONS FOR . . . TAKING A
SOCIAL MEDIA *detox*

- ☐ MY CRUSH MIGHT MISS MY ONLINE PRESENCE, AND THEY SAY ABSENCE MAKES THE HEART GROW FONDER.

- ☐ IT MIGHT MAKE ME SEEM MORE MYSTERIOUS (WHEN I'M ACTUALLY JUST BORED AT HOME).

- ☐ SO I CAN GET MORE BEAUTY REST– CLEAN SLEEPING, AND ALL THAT.

- ☐ TO WORK ON A NEW SOCIAL-MEDIA STRATEGY THAT'LL MAKE ME INSTA-FAMOUS.

- ☐ I'M GOING ON VACAY SOMEWHERE COMPLETELY AMAZING BUT TOTALLY DEVOID OF WI-FI.

- ☐ IT'S HARD WORK TYPING AND GETTING A MANICURE AT THE SAME TIME.

- ☐ THERE'S MORE TO LIFE THAN SOCIAL MEDIA (SOMETIMES I HAVE TO SHOP, TOO).

MY 10-POINT SOCIAL MEDIA DETOX PLAN

1. HAVE A SHORT RANT ABOUT HOW **I COULD QUIT** IT IF I WANTED TO.

2. REALIZE HOW HELPLESS I AM WHEN MY **PHONE BATTERY** DIES.

3. STOP BEING IN *denial* AND **ACCEPT** THE NEED FOR A DETOX.

4. **LOCK UP** ALL DEVICES. (BUILD A FARADAY CAGE IF I HAVE TO.)

5. FEEL UNJUSTIFIABLY **SMUG** ABOUT MY WHOLESOME **NEW** LIFE.

COMPLETE THE PLAN HERE.

6. _____

_____

7. _____

_____

8. _____

_____

9. _____

_____

10. HEAR THAT *Beyoncé* HAS DROPPED A **NEW** ALBUM AND IMMEDIATELY **GIVE UP** SO I CAN DOWNLOAD IT **BEFORE** ALL OF MY FRIENDS.

THINGS I CAN DO TO MAKE SURE PEOPLE DON'T MISS MY ONLINE PRESENCE TOO MUCH:

- ☐ MAKE A NOTE OF **EVERYTHING** I EAT, WEAR, THINK, AND SAY, AND THEN *send* IT TO PEOPLE. PEOPLE LOVE GETTING MAIL.

- ☐ LEAVE **HASHTAGS** ON **STICKY NOTES** AT PEOPLE'S HOUSES. FOR EXAMPLE, #TBT ON MY PARENTS' WEDDING PHOTO.

- ☐ _____
  ADD MORE HERE.
  _____

- ☐ _____
  _____

- ☐ _____
  _____

- ☐ _____
  _____

#MISSMEYET?

DELVING INTO MY DIVA HISTORY

HOW OLD I WAS WHEN I . . .

REALIZED I WAS *fabulous*: _____

DOWNLOADED MY FIRST SONG: _____

STARTING EARNING MONEY: _____

WENT TO MY FIRST CONCERT: _____

HAD MY *first kiss*: _____

HAD MY FIRST HEARTBREAK: _____

#OLDSCHOOL

THIS WAS MY LAST . . .

#THROWBACK

SELFIE: _____

PURCHASE: _____

GOOGLE SEARCH: _____

FLIRTATION: _____

TEXT SENT, AND WHAT IT *said*: _____

_____

PHOTO TAKEN, AND WHERE IT WAS: _____

BUT THIS WAS THE LAST TIME I...

SLEPT **PAST** NOON: _____

TURNED OFF MY PHONE: _____

ATE *my weight* IN CHOCOLATE: _____

TOLD SOMEONE I *loved* THEM: _____

DRAMATICALLY DIAGNOSED MYSELF
USING **SYMPTOMS** I FOUND **ONLINE**: _____

#TOTALHONESTY

AND THIS WAS THE LAST...

THING I **LIKED** ONLINE: _____

BOOK I READ: _____

COUNTRY I VISITED: _____

SERIES I **BINGE-WATCHED**: _____

SONG I **SUNG MY** *heart* **OUT** TO: _____

SARCASTIC COMMENT I MADE: _____

#TELLMEABOUTIT

DELVING INTO MY DIVA PRESENT

MY MOOD IN DOODLE FORM:

#NOWISTHENEWLATER

MY GOOD BOOKS:

IN

OUT

EWW, feelings...

RATE THESE SITUATIONS ON A SCALE OF 0-3.
0 MARKS MEANS IT'S *totally cool*, AND 3 MEANS IT'S A *meltdown*.
THEN ADD THE NUMBERS UP AND CHECK THE *diva* THERMOMETER.

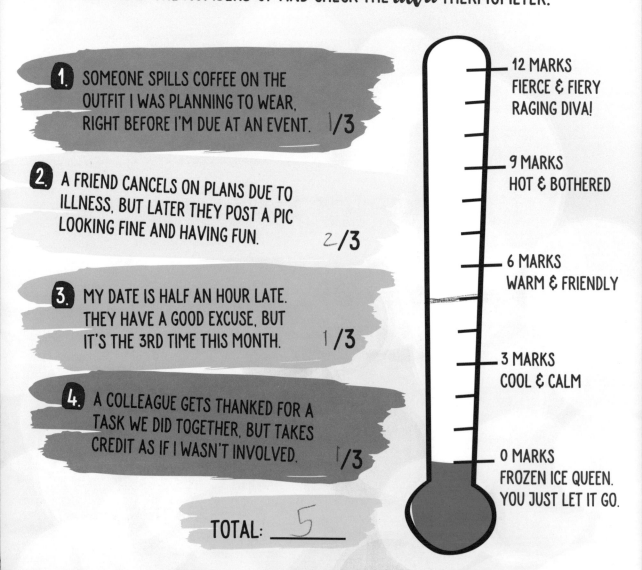

1. SOMEONE SPILLS COFFEE ON THE OUTFIT I WAS PLANNING TO WEAR, RIGHT BEFORE I'M DUE AT AN EVENT. 1/3

2. A FRIEND CANCELS ON PLANS DUE TO ILLNESS, BUT LATER THEY POST A PIC LOOKING FINE AND HAVING FUN. 2/3

3. MY DATE IS HALF AN HOUR LATE. THEY HAVE A GOOD EXCUSE, BUT IT'S THE 3RD TIME THIS MONTH. 1/3

4. A COLLEAGUE GETS THANKED FOR A TASK WE DID TOGETHER, BUT TAKES CREDIT AS IF I WASN'T INVOLVED. 1/3

TOTAL: 5

12 MARKS
FIERCE & FIERY
RAGING DIVA!

9 MARKS
HOT & BOTHERED

6 MARKS
WARM & FRIENDLY

3 MARKS
COOL & CALM

0 MARKS
FROZEN ICE QUEEN.
YOU JUST LET IT GO.

DELVING INTO MY DIVA FUTURE

WHICH OF THESE #GOALS IS MOST IMPORTANT TO ME?

- ☐ RELATIONSHIP GOALS
- ☐ SQUAD GOALS
- ☑ CAREER GOALS
- ☐ FITNESS GOALS

WHERE DO I SEE MYSELF IN 15 YEARS?

_____

_____

HOW *fabulous* DOES IT LOOK, ON A SCALE OF 1-10? _____

WHICH THINGS ARE KEY TO MAKING THAT FUTURE *a reality:*

- ☐ RAGING AMBITION
- ☐ CAFFEINE, IN A DRIP
- ☐ EXTREMELY HIGH STANDARDS
- ☐ MAKING MY FIRST MILLION
- ☐ UNFAILING SELF-CONFIDENCE
- ☐ A PERSONAL ASSISTANT
- ☐ AN ARMY OF MINIONS
- ☐ DIVA DETERMINATION

DIVAS DON'T LIKE WAITING . . .
NOT EVEN FOR THE **FUTURE.**
HERE'S A LIST OF **ALL** THE THINGS **I'M IMPATIENT** FOR:

_____

_____

_____

_____

I'M NOT HERE TO BE
AVERAGE:
I'M HERE TO BE
AWESOME.

#TRUTH

THINGS A *girl* NEEDS TO >>>

#SLAYALLDAY

_____

_____

_____

_____

_____

_____

_____

_____

_____

I'LL CONQUER *the world* AND **LOOK GOOD** DOING IT

ADD MORE HERE.

WITH THESE **DIVA** ESSENTIALS:

- ☐ A GREAT PAIR OF SHOES
- ☐ A WEEKLY MANI/PEDI
- ☐ A VOLUMINOUS BLOW-DRY
- ☐ A CAPSULE WARDROBE
- ☐ AN INTEREST-FREE CREDIT CARD!

- ☐ _____
- ☐ _____
- ☐ _____
- ☐ _____
- ☐ _____

BUT IF I COULD CHOOSE **ONE** OF THESE *fantasy* **"CHEATS,"** IT'D BE:

- ☐ A GOOD HAIR DAY, EVERY DAY
- ☐ UNBREAKABLE NAILS
- ☐ CALORIE-FREE CHOCOLATE
- ☐ CREASE-RESISTANT CLOTHES
- ☐ A PERSONAL MASSEUSE

- ☐ _____
- ☐ _____
- ☐ _____
- ☐ _____
- ☐ _____

My fantasy

"IF I WAS A **BILLIONAIRE**"

SHOPPING LIST

_____

_____

_____

_____

_____

_____

_____

_____

_____

BUT, FOR RICHER OR **POORER**, I'VE ALWAYS GOT . . .
★ ★ ★ ★ ★

_____

_____

_____

_____

_____

_____

_____

_____

_____

_____

_____

#THINGSMONEYCAN'TBU

#HIDDENDEPTHS

#NOTSOSHALLOW

MY KIND OF **MATH** PROBLEMS

I BUY A PACK OF **100 HAIR TIES** AT THE START OF THE MONTH AND BY THE END OF THE MONTH THERE IS *only* **ONE LEFT** AROUND MY WRIST . . . WHERE DID THE **OTHER 99 GO?**

_____

TWO SOCKS WENT INTO THE WASH, BUT ONLY **ONE** CAME OUT. *HOW?*

_____

I HAVE THE SAME NUMBER OF HOURS A DAY AS *Beyoncé*. I SLEEP FOR 8 HOURS, WORK FOR 8 HOURS, AND HAVE TO DO **BORING ADULT STUFF** FOR ANOTHER 7. HOW DO I BECOME AS **FIERCE** AS *Queen Bey* IN THE TIME LEFT OVER?

_____

I ATE **2 BARS OF CHOCOLATE** TONIGHT. THAT'S **1 MORE** THAN THIS MORNING. HOW MUCH CHOCOLATE HAVE I EATEN TODAY? AND HOW MUCH DO I *actually* CARE?

_____

A DIVA'S GUIDE TO:

friendship

A.K.A.
"MY CLIQUE-TIONARY"

- **B.A.E.** – THE PERSON I PUT BEFORE ANYONE ELSE

- **FAM** – FRIENDS SO CLOSE THEY'RE BASICALLY FAMILY

- **F.O.M.O.** – WHAT I FEEL WHEN MY FAM GOES OUT WITHOUT ME

- **P.L.U.** – PEOPLE LIKE US (AWESOME, OBVIOUSLY)

- **TRIBE** – A GROUP OF P.L.U. THAT STICK TOGETHER

- **SQUAD** – THOSE CHOSEN TO BE MY INNER CIRCLE

- **RIDE-OR-DIE** – THE BESTIE I'D DO ANYTHING FOR

- **FRENEMY** – A FRIEND WHO'S ALSO SECRETLY A RIVAL

MY REAL-LIFE **SQUAD:**

_____

_____

_____

_____

_____

MY *fantasy* **SQUAD:**

(WOULDN'T EVERYONE BE FRIENDS WITH **J-LAW** IF THEY COULD?)

We're besties.
IF YOU FALL,
I'LL BE THERE TO PICK
YOU UP . . . .

#AFTERIFINISHLAUGHING

THEY SAY YOUR

vibe

ATTRACTS YOUR

TRIBE.

SO I MUST BE GIVING OFF

SOME *pretty*

AMAZING

VIBES, RIGHT?

#ILOVEUS #BESTIES #FRIENDSFORLIFE

THE MOST **IMPORTANT** ELEMENTS
OF ANY *squad:*

- ☐ BEING ABLE TO BE BRUTALLY HONEST WITH EACH OTHER

- ☐ BEING ABLE TO CRACK EACH OTHER UP WITH ONE WORD OR LOOK

- ☐ BEING ABLE TO SILENTLY BINGE-WATCH NETFLIX TOGETHER

- ☐ BEING READY TO PARTY, WHENEVER, WHEREVER

- ☐ BEING ABLE TO TOLERATE EACH OTHER'S DIVA TENDENCIES

- ☐ BEING THERE WITH A SHOULDER TO CRY ON WHEN IT'S NEEDED MOST

- ☐ BEING ABLE TO HAVE DEEP AND MEANINGFUL CHATS FOR HOURS

- ☐ BEING WILLING TO CHECK EACH OTHER'S TEETH FOR GREEN BITS

- ☐ SHARING CLOTHES SO REGULARLY WE FORGET WHOSE ARE WHOSE

- ☐ HAVING EACH OTHER'S BACKS THROUGH THICK AND THIN

- ☐ HAVING ONE MAMA-HEN FRIEND WHO ORGANIZES EVERYONE

THAT MOMENT WHEN . . .

I SEND A
PRIVATE MESSAGE
TO A
group chat
INSTEAD.

#CRINGE
#AWKIES
#DELETE

3 TIMES I WISHED THE GROUND HAD **OPENED UP** AND SWALLOWED ME, AND HOW I *"styled"* IT OUT:

1.
_____
_____
_____
_____
_____

2.
_____
_____
_____
_____
_____

3.
_____
_____
_____
_____
_____

MY **MOST** EMBARRASSING SOCIAL FAUX PAS **EVER**

DESTROY PAGE AFTER WRITING!

IT'S *my party* AND I'LL **CRY** IF **I** <u>WANT</u> TO.

TIME TO CHOOSE: **CRY**, DENY, OR *fly* THROUGH THESE **TRICKY** SOCIAL SITUATIONS.

1. SOMEONE TURNS UP **UNINVITED** TO A MOVIE NIGHT I ORGANIZED. I HANDLE THIS BY . . .

CRY – ASKING *who* INVITED THEM. SOMEONE HAS BLURTED OUT THE DETAILS OF THE GATHERING WITHOUT **MY PERMISSION**. **HOW DARE THEY!** NOBODY LEAVES UNTIL I FIND THE TRAITOR.

DENY – *Pretending* I INVITED THEM AND **TAKING THE CREDIT** WHEN PEOPLE ENJOY THE CRASHER'S COMPANY. I CAN'T HAVE **ANYONE** QUESTIONING MY AUTHORITY!

Fly – WELCOMING THEM WITH **OPEN ARMS**. MY GATHERING IS OBVIOUSLY THE *highlight* OF THE SOCIAL CALENDAR.

2. I'VE DOUBLE-BOOKED **TWO** BIG EVENTS ON THE SAME NIGHT, NEITHER OF WHICH I WANT TO MISS. WHAT'S A DIVA TO DO?

CRY – WHAT A **DISASTER!** I'M SO WORRIED THAT ONE HOST WILL FIND OUT I CHOSE THE OTHER THAT I CANCEL BOTH AND MISS OUT ON ALL THE FUN.

DENY – I'LL HAVE *my cake* AND *eat it* TOO! I SHOW MY FACE AT BOTH EVENTS – THEY ARE ONLY A SHORT UBER RIDE AWAY FROM EACH OTHER.

Fly – I PICK **ONE** AND STICK TO IT. THAT JUST COMES WITH THE TERRITORY WHEN YOU'RE AS IN-DEMAND AS I AM. **MASSIVE** *apologies* TO THE RUNNER-UP!

3. I TELL **EVERYONE** I'M HAVING A **HUGE** PARTY, BUT IT TURNS OUT *only 10* PEOPLE CAN ATTEND!

CRY – THIS IS SOCIAL SUICIDE! I MIGHT AS WELL CANCEL THE **WHOLE** FLIPPING THING!

DENY – I'LL PRETEND I SAID "HYGGE" NOT "HUGE," AND IT WAS *always* MEANT TO BE A SMALL, SCANDI-STYLE GATHERING!

Fly – I QUICKLY CHANGE THE DATE SO MORE PEOPLE CAN COME. **I WON'T TOLERATE** PEOPLE FEELING SORRY FOR ME!

4. IT'S THE DAY BEFORE *Valentine's* AND I JUST GOT **DUMPED!** WHAT AM I GOING TO DO NOW?

CRY – SOB **ANGRILY** INTO MY PILLOW ALL NIGHT AND *potentially* BURN SOME OF MY EX'S THINGS.

DENY – **IGNORE IT** AND ASK MY EX'S BEST FRIEND OUT. I ALREADY HAVE A RESERVATION. **I REFUSE** TO BE SAD!

Fly – IT'S THEIR **LOSS!** I'LL CELEBRATE LOVE BY HOSTING A DINNER PARTY FOR MY **SINGLE** FRIENDS INSTEAD!

MOSTLY **CRYING** OVER SPILLED MILK

I NEED TO BE KINDER TO MYSELF AND ACCEPT THAT THINGS WON'T ALWAYS GO MY WAY. I ALSO NEED TO KEEP MY COOL WITH PEOPLE – IT'S NOT WORTH GETTING UPSET!

MOSTLY TOTALLY IN **DENIAL**

FAILURE IS NOT AN OPTION FOR ME, BUT I SHOULD TRY TO BE MORE UPFRONT WITH PEOPLE WHEN I ENCOUNTER PROBLEMS. I'M ONLY HUMAN. TRUE FRIENDS WON'T JUDGE!

MOSTLY A **SOCIAL** BUTTER*FLY*

LIFE IS TOO SHORT FOR DRAMA! THE TRUTH CAN HURT SOMETIMES, BUT PEOPLE KNOW WHERE THEY STAND WITH ME. I AM RELIABLY COOL, CALM, COLLECTED, AND HONEST!

REASONS FOR CANCELING A PLAN ★ ★ AT THE LAST-MINUTE

TIMES I HAVE CANCELED LAST-MINUTE:

IT'S A "NO" FROM ME WHEN:

- [ ] THERE'S A NEW SERIES ON NETFLIX
- [ ] I'D RATHER BE IN BED ALL DAY
- [ ] I'VE HAD A BETTER OFFER
- [ ] I'VE SPENT ALL MY MONEY
- [ ] IT'S RAINING AND COLD
- [ ] MY BESTIE CAN'T GO
- [ ] MY WORST FRENEMY IS GOING
- [ ] IT'LL TAKE ME OVER 30 MINUTES TO GET THERE
- [ ] _____
- [ ] _____
- [ ] _____
- [ ] _____

HERE ARE SOME **READY-MADE** EXCUSES
FOR WHEN I'M FEELING **FLAKY**:

1. I DON'T WANT TO RUN INTO ANY OF MY **MANY ADMIRERS**.

2. I ALREADY WORE MY *best outfit* ONCE THIS WEEK, AND I **CAN'T** BE SEEN IN AN INFERIOR LOOK.

3. I'M BUSY RUNNING A CROWDFUNDING **CAMPAIGN** FOR MY *extravagant* LIFESTYLE.

4. I MIGHT GET SPOTTED BY A **MODELING** SCOUT, AND I'M **NOT SURE** I'M READY FOR *fame* YET.

5. _____

ADD MORE HERE.

6. _____

#SORRYNOTSORRY

A DIVA'S GUIDE TO:

LOVE

AND

dating

(IT CAN'T BE THAT HARD, RIGHT?)

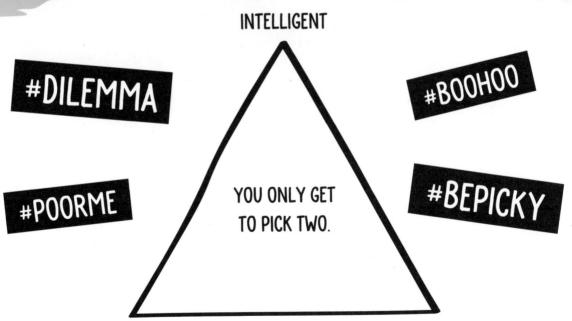

INTELLIGENT

#DILEMMA

#BOOHOO

#POORME

#BEPICKY

YOU ONLY GET TO PICK TWO.

EMOTIONALLY MATURE

GOOD-LOOKING

MY IDEAL PARTNER . . .

TALL **OR** SHORT?

LONG HAIR **OR** SHORT HAIR?

COOL AND CASUAL **OR** DRESSED TO IMPRESS?

INTROVERT **OR** EXTROVERT?

ARTISTICALLY MESSY **OR** TOTAL NEAT FREAK?

WELL-READ **OR** WELL-KNOWN?

TECH WHIZZ **OR** OLD-SCHOOL?

DOG LOVER **OR** CAT LOVER?

CITY DWELLER **OR** OUTDOORSY TYPE?

EARLY RISER **OR** NIGHT OWL?

DOES THIS PERSON EXIST IN REAL LIFE?

ARE THEY ALREADY IN MY *life?*

IF SO, WHAT AM I WAITING FOR?

#GOFORIT

DIVA DATING APPLICATION FORM #1

MOST JOBS REQUIRE AN INTERVIEW PROCESS. I HAVE TO *wonder* WHY WE DON'T DO THIS FOR *relationships?* PICKING A PARTNER CAN BE ONE OF THE HARDEST JOBS ON EARTH! USE THIS COMPREHENSIVE APPLICATION FORM ON A *crush* BEFORE OFFERING THEM THE POSITION OF A *lifetime.*

1. NAME:

_____

3. D.O.B.:

_____

4. ZIP CODE:

_____

5. CAR REGISTRATION NUMBER:

_____

2. QUICK SELF-PORTRAIT:

6. HOBBIES AND INTERESTS:

_____

_____

7. SKILLS:

_____

_____

8. **RELATIONSHIP** HISTORY:

_____

_____

9. REASON FOR **ENDING** YOUR LAST RELATIONSHIP:

_____

_____

10. DO YOU STILL TALK TO YOUR **EX?**   YES / NO

11. IS YOUR **MOTHER** A SOCIOPATH?   YES / NO

12. ARE YOU LIKELY TO **FREAK OUT** AT THE MENTION OF **ANY** OF THE FOLLOWING THINGS (PLEASE CIRCLE):

MARRIAGE   CHILDREN   SPIDERS

13. ARE YOU LIKELY TO **BREAK UP** WITH ME IF I:

A) STOP SHAVING MY LEGS   YES / NO

B) GAIN WEIGHT DURING THE HOLIDAY SEASON   YES / NO

C) WEAR MY BIGGEST GRANNY PANTS   YES / NO

14. HAVE THE FOLLOWING WORDS **EVER** LEFT YOUR MOUTH TO ANY FEMALE **EVER:** *"Is it that time of the month or something?"*

YES / NO

ASSESSOR'S COMMENTS: _____

_____

_____

DIVA DATING APPLICATION FORM #2

1. NAME:

_____

2. QUICK SELF-PORTRAIT:

3. D.O.B.:

_____

4. ZIP CODE:

_____

5. CAR REGISTRATION NUMBER:

_____

6. HOBBIES AND INTERESTS:

_____

_____

7. SKILLS:

_____

_____

8. RELATIONSHIP HISTORY:

_____

_____

9. REASON FOR ENDING YOUR LAST RELATIONSHIP:

_____

_____

10. DO YOU STILL TALK TO YOUR EX?   YES / NO

11. IS YOUR **MOTHER** A SOCIOPATH?   YES / NO

12. ARE YOU LIKELY TO **FREAK OUT** AT THE MENTION OF **ANY** OF THE FOLLOWING THINGS (PLEASE CIRCLE):

MARRIAGE   CHILDREN   SPIDERS

13. ARE YOU LIKELY TO **BREAK UP** WITH ME IF I:

A) STOP SHAVING MY LEGS   YES / NO

B) GAIN WEIGHT DURING THE HOLIDAY SEASON   YES / NO

C) WEAR MY BIGGEST GRANNY PANTS   YES / NO

14. HAVE THE FOLLOWING WORDS **EVER** LEFT YOUR MOUTH TO ANY FEMALE **EVER**: *"Is it that time of the month or something?"*

YES / NO

ASSESSOR'S COMMENTS: _____

_____

_____

BE AS **PICKY** WITH YOUR *love life* AS YOU ARE WITH YOUR **SELFIES**

#LOVE

#YOURSELF

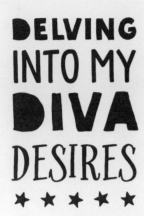

DELVING INTO MY DIVA DESIRES
★ ★ ★ ★ ★

MY ULTIMATE *crush*...

WHEN I WAS IN ELEMENTARY SCHOOL:

_____

THAT I'VE ALWAYS KEPT *secret*:

_____

ON A FRIEND'S SIBLING:

_____

IN THE *music* INDUSTRY:

_____

IN THE SPORTS INDUSTRY:

_____

IN *Hollywood*:

_____

WHOSE **NAME** I DON'T KNOW:

_____

WHAT DO ALL THESE *crushes* HAVE IN COMMON?

THE TRAITS I FIND
most attractive...

RATE THEIR IMPORTANCE OUT OF 10.

CONFIDENCE	/10	PASSION	/10
SENSITIVITY	/10	INTEGRITY	/10
KINDNESS	/10	LOYALTY	/10
THOUGHTFULNESS	/10	CREATIVITY	/10
INTELLIGENCE	/10	AMBITION	/10
SENSE OF HUMOR	/10	COCKINESS	/10

TOP 5 SONGS
THAT MAKE ME FEEL
EXTRA flirty:

1. _____
2. _____
3. _____
4. _____
5. _____

THE perfect DATE...

PLAN THE ULTIMATE DATE HERE.
DREAM UP AN IDEAL DAY OUT AND
MAKE EVERY MINUTE COUNT.

IF YOU CAN'T **HANDLE** ME AT MY *worst,* YOU DON'T *deserve* ME AT MY **BEST.**

— MARILYN MONROE
(A.K.A. DIVA QUEEN)

IS DATING ME **DIFFICULT**, DEMANDING, OR *drama-filled?* LET'S TAKE A REALITY CHECK.

1. ON A **BLIND DATE**, I AM LIKELY TO BE . . .

A) SUPER EARLY, SO I CAN BRIEF THE RESTAURANT STAFF ON MY BAILOUT SIGNAL.

B) PUNCTUAL. I WOULDN'T WANT MY DATE TO BE LATE, SO WHY SHOULD I BE?

c) *Fashionably late.* I LET THEM SWEAT BEFORE I SAUNTER IN ALL **RELAXED** AND COOL.

2 ON OUR **SECOND DATE** I AM LIKELY TO BE . . .

A) SURPRISED WE MADE IT THIS FAR.

B) PAYING FOR THE BILL. IT'S ONLY FAIR – THEY PAID LAST TIME.

c) ORDERING *lobster* (SINCE THEY'LL BE PAYING AGAIN).

3 I KNOW THERE'S A *spark* BETWEEN US WHEN . . .

A) THEY MANAGE TO MAKE THIS COLD-HEARTED *ice queen* SMILE.

B) I'M **SO** ENGAGED, I'M NOT EVEN TEMPTED TO CHECK MY PHONE.

c) THEY **HAVEN'T** MENTIONED THEIR MOTHER, SISTER, OR EX YET!

4. I'M READY TO INVITE THEM TO **MY PLACE** WHEN . . .

A) MY ROOMMATE HAS HAD A CHANCE TO INTERROGATE THEM. A SECOND OPINION IS **ESSENTIAL.**

B) I'VE DONE MY **MONTHLY CLEANING,** AND THE PLACE LOOKS OKAY. NO TIME LIKE THE PRESENT.

C) MY FRIDGE CONTAINS **EVERYTHING** NEEDED FOR BREAKFAST . . . JUST IN CASE.

5. THEY'RE INVITED TO MEET MY **PARENTS** WHEN . . .

A) I'VE HAD A CHANCE TO *restyle* THEM AND THEY'RE LOOKING REASONABLY PRESENTABLE.

B) WE'VE BEEN **SEEN** OUT IN PUBLIC AND THE CAT'S OUT OF THE BAG ANYWAY.

C) I'VE RUN OUT OF **MONEY** BUT I'D LOVE A GOOD DINNER – IT'S CHEAPER THAN A DATE!

6. I AM READY TO DROP THE *L-word* WHEN . . .

A) THEY'VE SAID IT **FIRST.**

B) THEY'VE **PROVEN** THEY CAN DO THE DISHES AND PICK UP AFTER THEMSELF.

C) THEY'VE BROUGHT ME *flowers* FOR NO REASON.

MOSTLY A's =
HEART OF STONE

I'M DIFFICULT TO DATE, BUT ONLY BECAUSE
I REFUSE TO SETTLE FOR ANYTHING LESS THAN
PERFECT. I WON'T LET ANYONE INTO MY WORLD
UNTIL THEY'VE PROVED THEIR WORTHINESS. BUT
IF THEY DO SOMEHOW MANAGE TO PASS THE TEST,
I'LL BE FIERCELY LOYAL AND LOVING.

MOSTLY B's =
Romantic realist

I EXPECT A LOT OF MYSELF AND DEMAND
THE SAME FROM MY DATES. WE'LL SPLIT
THE BILL, DRESS TO IMPRESS, AND HOLD LIVELY
CONVERSATIONS – BUT IF THEY FAIL TO CALL
OR TEXT ME WITHIN THE APPROPRIATE
TIME FRAME, THEY'LL BE DROPPED.
ALL'S FAIR IN LOVE AND WAR!

MOSTLY C's =
TOTAL HANDFUL

IN THE WORDS OF TAYLOR SWIFT, "BABY,
I'M A NIGHTMARE DRESSED LIKE A DAYDREAM."
I'LL HAVE YOU HANGING ON MY EVERY WORD AND
JUMPING THROUGH HOOPS, BUT THE TRUTH IS, I'M
NOT LOOKING FOR ANYTHING SERIOUS. I'M HAVING
WAY TOO MUCH FUN PLAYING THE FIELD!

DELVING INTO MY DIVA DATING LIFE
★ ★ ★ ★ ★

MY LIST OF PAST loves:

_____

_____

_____

_____

_____

MY NEW romantic INTEREST IS ANXIOUS TO MOVE FORWARD BUT **SOMETHING** IS HOLDING ME BACK. HERE ARE ALL THE PROS AND CONS:

PROS

CONS

#WHATAMIWAITINGFOR?

IF SOMETHING IS IMPORTANT TO ME, MUST IT BE
IMPORTANT TO THEM? IF YES, LIST THE NONNEGOTIABLES:

_____

_____

_____

_____

_____

#NOTMEANTTOBE

BUT I'M NOT UNREASONABLE. I'M OPEN TO
NEGOTIATIONS ON THESE MATTERS:

_____

_____

_____

_____

#MAYBEBABY

FIVE MESSAGES AND WHAT THEY **MEAN**. BE WARNED: THIS IS GOING TO **SUCK**.

HEY, I'M **REALLY BUSY** WITH **WORK** RIGHT NOW; I'LL **CATCH UP** WITH YOU **SOON**.

EVERYONE GETS A LUNCH BREAK AND IS ALLOWED TO GO TO THE BATHROOM. IT'S *illegal* TO WORK ALL WEEK WITH **NO BREAK!** IF THEY CAN'T FIND THE TIME TO MESSAGE **ME**, THEY'RE JUST **NOT THAT INTO IT**.

WE SHOULD **DEFINITELY** HANG OUT **SOON**. DROP ME A LINE **NEXT WEEK** AND I'LL SEE WHAT **MY SCHEDULE** LOOKS LIKE.

I **DON'T** NEED TO EXPLAIN THIS ONE! ORGANIZING TO **MEET UP** INCLUDES THE FOLLOWING *details*: DAY, TIME, AND PLACE. IF THEY **WANT** TO SEE ME, THEY'LL MAKE A **PLAN**.

HI, SORRY I DIDN'T TEXT YOU BACK. WHAT ARE YOU DOING RIGHT NOW?

SENT AT 11PM.

NO MESSAGE BEFORE 7, NO DATE AFTER 11 . . . IT'S A SIMPLE RULE TO PLAY BY. IF I CAN'T HAVE THEIR EVENING, THEY DON'T DESERVE *my night!*

HEY, CAN I BRING A FRIEND? I THINK YOU'D REALLY LIKE THEM.

UH-OH. THEY MUST NOT SEE ME IN A *romantic* WAY. THREE'S A CROWD . . . UNLESS THE PERSON THEY'RE TRYING TO SET ME UP WITH IS HOT!

NO TEXT AT ALL . . .

IT'S NOT A MISTAKE: THEY GENUINELY HAVEN'T MESSAGED. THAT MEANS THEY'RE UNINTERESTED OR BUSY TEXTING OTHER PEOPLE. FORGET THAT *I-know-you've-been-online* MESSAGE AND JUST DELETE THEM!

WHEN MY TEXT HAS BEEN **READ** BUT NOT **REPLIED TO.**

★ ★ ★ ★ ★

MIPHONE PROBS #4

WAYS TO DEAL WITH PEOPLE WHO **AREN'T** PAYING ME ENOUGH **ATTENTION:**

1. _____
2. _____
3. _____
4. _____
5. _____

SOMETIMES YOU HAVE TO **"UNFOLLOW"** PEOPLE IN **REAL LIFE.**

A DIVA'S GUIDE TO:

Adulting

(CHORES, WORK, FINANCES, AND ALL THAT OTHER STUFF)

BEING **FEROCIOUSLY** AMBITIOUS BUT TOO *fabulous* TO LIFT A FINGER IS HAAAAAARD.

WHEN IT COMES TO GETTING **STUFF DONE**, TRY THIS A, B, C, D-IVA PRIORITIZATION METHOD.

ACTUALLY HAVE TO DO IT

BETTER GET ON WITH IT

COULD LEAVE THIS A LITTLE WHILE LONGER

DEFINITELY DON'T CARE ABOUT THIS AT ALL

My TO DO list

DO IT **NOW**.

DO IT LATER.

DO IT MUCH **LATER**.

DO IT MUCH, MUUUUCH **LATER**.

IGNORE IT UNTIL IT GOES AWAY.

THINGS I'LL **NEVER** GET AROUND TO:

_____

_____

_____

_____

_____

_____

#NOTINTHISLIFETIME

#PROCRASTINATION

#NOTNOW #NOTEVER

A VENN DIAGRAM DEPICTING MY CURRENT ADULTING SITCH:

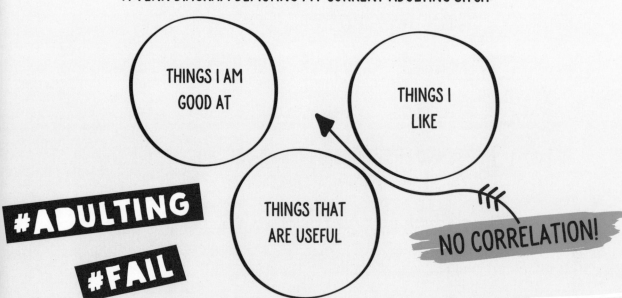

THINGS I AM
GOOD AT

THINGS I
LIKE

THINGS THAT
ARE USEFUL

NO CORRELATION!

#ADULTING

#FAIL

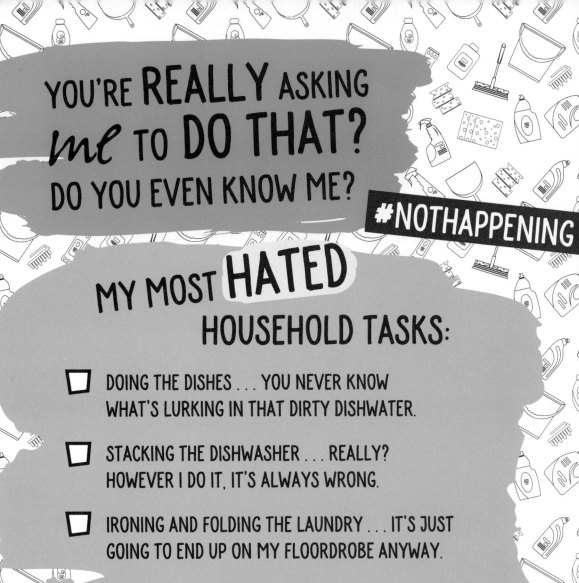

YOU'RE **REALLY** ASKING *me* TO **DO THAT?** DO YOU EVEN KNOW ME?

#NOTHAPPENING

MY MOST **HATED** HOUSEHOLD TASKS:

- ☐ DOING THE DISHES . . . YOU NEVER KNOW WHAT'S LURKING IN THAT DIRTY DISHWATER.

- ☐ STACKING THE DISHWASHER . . . REALLY? HOWEVER I DO IT, IT'S ALWAYS WRONG.

- ☐ IRONING AND FOLDING THE LAUNDRY . . . IT'S JUST GOING TO END UP ON MY FLOORDROBE ANYWAY.

- ☐ TAKING THE TRASH OUT . . . NOPE.

- ☐ VACUUMING . . . IT TOTALLY SUCKS.

- ☐ DUSTING THE BOOKSHELVES . . . WHY DO YOU THINK I BOUGHT AN E-READER?

- ☐ WATERING THE PLANTS . . . I'M A SERIAL PLANTKILLER.

MY TOP TIPS FOR TASK-AVOIDANCE

1. PRETEND TO GO TO THE **BATHROOM.**

2. PRETEND TO BE **ASLEEP.**

3. PRETEND TO BE *sick.*

4. **DISAPPEAR** WITHOUT A TRACE.

ADD MORE HERE.

5. _____

6. _____

7. _____

8. _____

9. _____

10. _____

IF **MONDAY** WAS A ➤➤➤

haircut,

IT WOULD BE A

MULLET.

REASONS FOR **THROWING** ★·A SICKIE·★

- ☐ MY WORK-BESTIE IS SICK OR AWAY.
- ☐ I'M IGNORING A REALLY HUGE DEADLINE.
- ☐ MY CAR HAS BROKEN DOWN (AT THE MALL).
- ☐ I WAS PARTYING LAST NIGHT AND DIDN'T GET ANY BEAUTY SLEEP.
- ☐ I'M EATING MY WAY THROUGH A BREAK-UP (ICE CREAM STILL LOVES ME).
- ☐ I'M HAVING SURGERY (IF AN OMBRÉ HAIR-DYE JOB COUNTS AS SURGERY).
- ☐ BAD HAIRCUT . . . 'NUFF SAID.

THINGS I'D **RATHER** BE DOING THAN **GOING TO WORK:**

_____

_____

_____

_____

_____

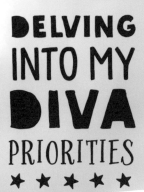

DELVING INTO MY DIVA PRIORITIES

★ ★ ★ ★ ★

ADULTING VS. TREATING MYSELF!

I'M DOWN TO EMERGENCY CASH.

WHICH IS IT TO BE . . .

BUYING GAS FOR MY CAR **OR** A KILLER PAIR OF PUMPS?

GROCERIES FOR THE WEEK **OR** ONE BIG MEAL OUT?

MY CELLPHONE BILL **OR** A NIGHT OUT WITH FRIENDS?

FIXING A LEAK IN MY ROOF **OR** SOME NEW SWIMWEAR?

PAYING A PARKING FINE **OR** GETTING A HAIRCUT?

I HAVE ONE DAY OFF. DO I SPEND IT . . .

VISITING FAMILY **OR** SLEEPING IN?

BABYSITTING FOR A FRIEND **OR** GOING TO THE SPA?

CLEANING THE HOUSE **OR** WATCHING NETFLIX?

WORKING ON A D.I.Y. PROJECT **OR** WORKING ON MY TAN?

SHOPPING FOR THINGS I NEED **OR** SHOPPING FOR THINGS I WANT?

I'M REALLY **TIRED**. DO I USE MY
LAST OUNCE OF *energy* FOR . . .

TAKING OUT THE TRASH **OR** WATCHING TRASHY TV?

COOKING DINNER **OR** ORDERING A PIZZA?

A NICE HOT SHOWER **OR** SHOWERING INSTAGRAM WITH SELFIES?

PLANNING TOMORROW'S OUTFIT **OR** LOOKING AT CELEB OUTFITS ONLINE?

CHECKING A NEWS WEBSITE **OR** DOING SOME ONLINE SHOPPING?

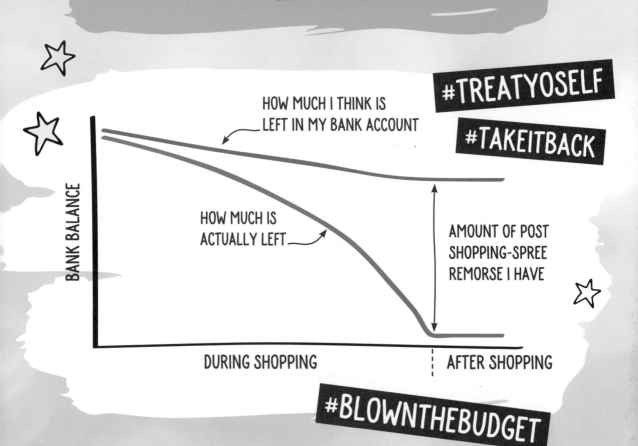

HOW MUCH I THINK IS
LEFT IN MY BANK ACCOUNT

#TREATYOSELF

#TAKEITBACK

HOW MUCH IS
ACTUALLY LEFT

AMOUNT OF POST
SHOPPING-SPREE
REMORSE I HAVE

BANK BALANCE

DURING SHOPPING   AFTER SHOPPING

#BLOWNTHEBUDGET

WHEN MY CELLPHONE IS ALMOST **DEAD**, **BUT I CAN'T BE BOTHERED** TO REACH MY **CHARGER** FROM **BED**.

#LOWKEYANNOYING

OTHER FIRST WORLD PROBLEMS:

1. WHEN I'M LAZING AROUND, LOOKING AT MY PHONE, AND I DROP IT ON MY FACE.

2. WHEN I PAY FOR A BLOW-DRY, AND THEN IMMEDIATELY GET CAUGHT IN A *rainstorm*.

3. WHEN MY PHONE BATTERY DIES OVERNIGHT, AND MY ALARM DOESN'T GO OFF.

4. WHEN THE ITEM I JUST BOUGHT GOES ON SALE, TWO DAYS LATER.

5. WHEN I OPEN MY *camera* IN REVERSE, AND SEE MYSELF FROM MY WORST ANGLE.

6. WHEN THE *barista* ACCIDENTALLY GIVES ME DECAF INSTEAD OF A DOUBLE SHOT.

APPS I'D INVENT TO ADULT FOR ME:

_____

_____

_____

_____

_____

_____

_____

_____

SHOULDN'T THERE BE **AN** **APP** FOR THIS?

#APP-RECIATION

WHEN I'M IN NEED OF A LITTLE R&R AFTER A BUSY WEEK OF adulting

THESE ITEMS MAKE THE
perfect PAMPER DAY.

- [ ] A REALLY, REALLY BUBBLY BATH
- [ ] A HOMEMADE MANI/PEDI
- [ ] A BOXSET OF MY FAVORITE SHOW
- [ ] THE ULTIMATE RELAXATION PLAYLIST
- [ ] A PINK UNICORN ONESIE
- [ ] A STOCKPILE OF DELICIOUS SNACKS
- [ ] A GLOSSY NEW MAGAZINE

- [ ] LOTS AND LOTS OF SCENTED CANDLES
- [ ] SNAPCHATTING MYSELF IN A FACEMASK
- [ ] A BESTSELLING NEW BOOK
- [ ] WEARING PANTS AROUND THE HOUSE
- [ ] HAVING MY HAIR UP IN A MESSY BUN
- [ ] SCROLLING THROUGH PINTEREST

#METIME
#PAMPERSESH

PICK A *pamper* DAY MANTRA:

ALL I WANT IS *world* PEACE . . . AND **PERFECT EYEBROWS.**

WHEN ALL ELSE **FAILS** . . . ➤ GET A MASSAGE.

treat *yo self*

LIFE ISN'T *perfect*, BUT YOUR *nails* **CAN BE.**

SLEEP WELL, *Princess*

TO BE AT MY *best*, IT'S **ESSENTIAL** TO GET
A GOOD NIGHT'S SLEEP. **DOODLE** THE WAY
TO *dreamland* ON THIS PAGE.

NOW, CLOSE THE BOOK AND *drift away* -
TOMORROW'S ANOTHER **DIVA DAY!**